First published 2011

ISBN : 978-1-906817-89-3

The publisher acknowledges subsidy from

ALBA | CHRUTHACHAIL

towards the publication of this book

The paper used in this book promotes sustainable forest
management and is PEFC credited material.

PEFC

Printed and bound by
Martins the Printers, Berwick Upon Tweed

Typeset in 10 point Quadraat
by 3btype.com

NeVeR MIND
THE CAPTIONS

ALISTAIR FINDLAY

Luath Press Limited

EDINBURGH

www.luath.co.uk

CONTENTS

ACKNOWLEDGEMENTS

Thanks are due to the Scottish Arts Council for funding towards publication.

Thanks also to the Directors of the Museums and Galleries involved for the access given to the following collections, exhibitions, national and civic monuments and to the artists and sculptors, dead and alive, whose work is included here:

The National Museum of Scotland
The Stirling Smith Art Gallery & Museum
The Kelvingrove Art Gallery & Museum
The Museum on the Mound
The People's Palace & Winter Garden
The Museum of Edinburgh
The Museum of the People's Story
The Museum of Childhood
Dumfries Museum & Camera Obscura
Summerlee Heritage Park, Coatbridge
Greenhill Covenanters' House, Biggar
St Giles Cathedral
The Gallery of Modern Art, Glasgow
The Scottish Parliament Building
Surgeons' Hall, Edinburgh
The Glasgow Police Museum
The Centre for Contemporary Arts
Robert Burns Birthplace Museum
Annet House, Linlithgow

The Scottish National Portrait Gallery
Old St Paul's Church, Edinburgh
Civic & Street Monuments
Museum of Women
Museum of the Mind

Thanks are due specifically to the following artists for the permission to use their work: Calum Colvin, Sandy Moffat, Timothy Neat, Shelagh Atkinson (www.shelaghatkinson.co.uk), as well as to Andrew Hillhouse and the other paintings taken from the Stirling Smith collection.

Thanks also to the Surgeons' Hall, Edinburgh, for the use of photographs taken by Max McKenzie

The poem 'The Five Sisters' previously appeared in *Sex, Death and Football* (2003), 'John Knox's Grave' and 'I am Elizabeth, John Knox's daughter' appeared in *The Love Songs of John Knox* (2006), and 'Michael McGahey's Portrait by Maggie Hambling' appeared in *For Angus* (ed. Richard Berengarten and Gideon Calder, Los Poetry Press, Cambridge, 2009).

An extensive note on 'sources' is provided at the end of the book.

For Gavin & Audrey MacDougall, Louise & Rupert

PREFACE

The idea that paintings and the characters depicted in them have stories of their own to tell, often absurd and unexpected, first came to my attention in the work of the Irish poet, Paul Durcan, who used paintings in the National Gallery of Ireland and the National Gallery in London to create the marvellously deranged monologues found in *Crazy About Women* and *Give Me Your Hand* respectively. From Bertolt Brecht's *War Primer*, which has photographs cut from newspapers and magazines documenting the rise of Fascism in the thirties, I noticed the way he placed four-line rhymed stanzas of verse beneath each picture giving his own terse, sometimes inflamed, commentary – plangent, dashed-off, dyspeptic, humane. Finally, I came across a collection of essays by Peter Vergo, editor of *The New Museology* (Reaktion Books, London, 1997), in which the following sentence simply leapt out and fired my imagination to the extent of devising this book (49): 'The notion that works of art, in particular, should be left to speak for themselves takes no account of the fact that such works are, for most visitors, remarkably taciturn objects.'

Since so much of writing, both critical and creative, is concerned with 'giving voice', it seemed to me possible that by bringing object, image and text together one might also stir up some of the discourses which normally surround such artefacts to create some fun and fascination and even the odd, unexpected insight, which is the hope of all art and writing.

Alistair Findlay
Bathgate, September 2011

beyond the captions
the information panels
the catalogues
the museum directors
the treasure chests
the prized objects
the spoils of war
victory, ownership, control
the domination of myth
lichen
you, the visitors

THE NATIONAL MONUMENT: CALTON HILL

It stands against the skyline
in bright mid-winter sun
like some great emblem from
the Wall of Antonine, 'Pax Scotorum',
the Imperial dream of Rome, well,
Victorian Edinburgh's idea of same,
of being Unbarbarian, North Briton.

I like the way it stops, half-built,
one end thrust out,
the rest just grass and air,
jutting northwards into space,
end-stopped by reality, and lack of funds,
as the legions were by the Grampians
and the last of the free.

I like the way it looks all ways at once,
north and south and east and west,
yet looks from here, from this place,
as though it had a mind to change.
To hell with upturned boats, symbols
of a modernity we already have
yet seem afraid to own.

Calton Hill Monument for the Napoleonic war dead, 1826–29
Charles Robert Cockerell 1788–1863

THE NATIONAL MUSEUM OF SCOTLAND

panels stairs glass
art history or rubble

these stones
cable-stitched along their edge

Pictish verse
or Ossian's granny's knitting

a scarf perhaps
or a metal clasp

battle-worn
the flimsiest of gauze

roars tears silence

Prehistoric jewellery placed on Early People sculptures
Sir Eduardo Paolozzi, 1924–2005

reticent objects
left to speak for themselves
are often remarkably taciturn
and often say very little
unless coaxed into eloquence

by the historian, art critic
girl in the museum shop

Carved stone with Pictish symbols c.700AD, Cadboll
History is silent on their meaning

Farewell, dwellers by the sea! We leave you
Ford Prefect, all the science of the universe
and a cure for cancer. You gave us your Chiefs'
daughters and a recipe for beer. You are THE PITS.

one small item
a prayer book, tiny
rich in lapsis, gold
exquisite in itself
unusual marginalia
in Medieval Latin
almost illegible
pharmacological in nature
a priestly hand
undoubtedly
a remedy for syphilis

Bronze figure of Christ from a crucifix found on Islay
Argyll, 13th century

I flutter here, unnailed, a flambéed Christ,
prayed upon, stickless, waiting amongst
the locusts and other delicacies Pilot likes.
He picks me up, opens wide his mouth.

the doorway
a case study

the problem of
its size, complexity

its concealed history
not in fact a doorway

but an archway into
a pseudo-medieval idiom

the exact reverse of
a period room, shop-fitting, company logo

Stonework from doorways at Jedburgh Abbey
12th–13th centuries

Welcome to the Scottish Parliament
the best wee parliament in the world
designed for Glasgow Corporation
rewired, Salmond of Saltoun

looted and not restituted
stolen works of art
raped countries of origin
plundered antiquities

Silver urns, 17th century
Scottish silversmiths were renowned for their craftsmanship

Dear Legatee of Thord the Yeller, sorry
we are unable to return your illustrious
ancestor's Danegeld, but it appears he
may have stolen it from another museum.

THE AXE FACTORY MANAGERS' CONVENTION

We come here every year with Viking Tours
– The Axe Factory Managers' Convention –
all square-dancing and eyes-bulging contests.
Look! That's me, the current world champion.

I'm standing beside Sigard the Unstable.
He won the Berserker of the Year Award
two years running, a big deal in these parts.
I miss Rowena, who died in the crowd-rush

for Eric Tornpants, the neolithic rock star,
when he beached at Skara Brae. War clouds
gather. Big Toamy, leader of the Flint
Knappers Union, will strike for the Two-Hour

Day, if they let him out of clink, that is.
They say there is a Wall down South to keep
the Romans out. Let them come! I care not,
the laverock sings, and Freya smiles on me.

Lewis Chessmen carved in the 12th century
probably Norwegian

THE STIRLING SMITH

rescued from the skip, the local
found claimed donated
this history, this people

this place of battle
the banner of Polmaise Colliery
the first out and solidest in 1984–5

unearthed, mud-stained, by dog-walkers
a huge wrought-iron mangle
hand-turned by girls in granite mansions

the beautiful, inlaid, intact
the tall grandfather clock, shipped-out
survived the hazardous voyage back from
   Newfoundland

this place of trumpets
blood sweat siege
held reclaimed fought for

against the forgetting

The Battle of Stirling Bridge, 2000
Andrew Hillhouse

in museums
everyone becomes a child

the sense of bewilderment
when invited to look at

a piece of pottery
a fragment of rock

without already knowing, precisely
what we are looking for

The Thieves' Fetter found beside
the Old Bridge of Stirling, 19th century

I believe that the people themselves
will work out their own emancipation
kicking off here a bolt, there a bar,
loosening their chains link by link.

RB CUNNINGHAME GRAHAM

an object can stand for
a whole essay on genealogy

Pipe of Freedom, c.1866, Thomas Stuart Smith (1814–69)
celebrating the abolition of slavery in America

Niggers who have no cannons have no rights,
their land, their cattle, possessions – ours,
their women ours to infect with syphilis,
leave with child, outrage, torment, make beasts.

RB CUNNINGHAME GRAHAM

a fascination with the way things work
rather than who works them and to what end

contradicts the history of ordinary people

Mangles, sinks 19th and 20th centuries

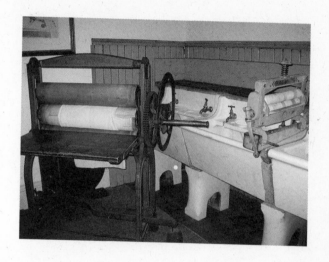

our homes are filled with things we own
rowing-machines we never exercise on
dining-tables we never eat at
triple-ovens we never cook in

the demand for a larger life
the experience of self-possession
self-making, emancipation

Bruce and de Bohun, the Stirling Smith
John Duncan (1866–1945)

Love of man placed before love of pelf,
plenty of work for all, no idle drones,
no machine slaves, take over what is yours,
the land and wealth, and manage it yourselves.

RB CUNNINGHAME GRAHAM

who made these
villeins serfs slaves
masters' apprentices

a workhouse child

objects too large
for the museum of childhood
to contain, own up to

Miss Annie Gillespie's wedding dress worn in 1742
Provost of Stirling's daughter

only wealthy women who did not work
could wear corsets then abandon them
as soon as they became the sign for
conventional values

THE CLYDE CLOCK

Time is running away from
Buchanan Street Bus Station,
with its trainers on, its shorts,
its athletic legs, running to,
past, out of, Time.

Time waits for no man
or woman or artist
or tide or bus, so the poets say,
how late the giro is, how late,
look at it go.

Time present is Time past,
the Sands of Time doth run,
etcetera, so, thanks very much, George,
for reminding us, Time is ticking away,
you old rascal, tick-tock, tick-tock, tick-

Clyde Clock/The Running Man, 2005
Buchanan Street Bus Station, George Wylie (b.1921)

THE KELVINGROVE

vertical sandstone building
tilted marble hall

an aircraft slowly circles
an organ madly plays

The carcase of an ox sings
There is a green hill far away

a man is shouting
he comes from Springburn

and doesn't need daft wee labels
telling him what to think

Return to Sender
1996, Sean Read

beyond the class system
hybrid publics

well-educated
high income families with children
young homeless
reduced income

fight the connoisseurs
the local anarchists
flocks of tourists
for access, space, hegemony

Display placard
I'm dead

I would rather make a thin living
in the arts at home
than strive towards a knighthood
in some imperial outpost

the history of the modern chair
has a lot to say about

the uncomfortable scar tissue
dividing design from art

The Heads, 2006
Sophy Cave

what every designer wants
is their name on a chair
or an adjustable lamp
not a camera, bike or website

the truth of cataloguing
of dating

the artist's handling
of paint

the fading colour
of paint

Girl Weeping over Her
Dead Canary

no longer yellow

The carcase of an ox, 1655
Rembrandt Harmensz van Rijn (1606–69)

their anatomy half-human, half-animal
confined in oddly proportioned space
we have no name for them
and no name for what we feel about them

a comprehensive display of coffins
the oldest loaf in the world
a man-powered flying machine
the remains of Julia Pastrana
(half-woman, half-baboon)

Vickers-Armstrong Supermarine Spitfire, 1944

the strafing of works of art
in pursuit of the pay claim
was the act of a lone militant
Pilots' Union

a football match
shopping

anything with weight
fragrance vibration

anything
rather than watch television

RB Cunninghame Graham, 1924
Jacob Epstein (1880–1959)

all the cares of life called civilised,
with all its littleness, its newspapers,
all full of nothing, its sordid aims disguised,
its hideous riches and its sordid poverty

RB CUNNINGHAME GRAHAM

and when I am in the boards
my words will be as a prophecy

and there will return the stock of the tenantry
who were driven over the sea

Silver trophy, International Race for First Class Yachts
Sir Thomas Lipton's *Shamrock*, 1901

And the 'beggars' of gentry
will be routed as they (the crofters) were
deer and sheep will be wheeled away
and the glens will be tilled

MARY MACPHERSON, 'BIG MARY OF THE SONGS'

DUST OR BUST

Where are all the busts of women,
you get my meaning, the civic monuments,
Delacroix's *Liberty Leading the People*,
Mother Courage dragging her cart across
the battlefields of Europe, Jenny Geddes,
loud and thrang, hurling her stool
amang the dunder-heids, the prelates?

If you Google 'female sculptures, Scots'
you get back 'Scottish female singers'
(seventy pages worth), while (538 pages)
The Public Sculpture of Glasgow says
the entrance hall of the Scottish Pavilion,
built by Basil Spence in 1938, portrays
a colossal female representing 'Service'.

On the pedestal, a relief of a naked girl,
standing on a vesica-shaped letter 'O'
– ie 'a urinary bladder' – O yes, and,
on the outside walls, the statues of 'great
Scots', Burns *et al.* I texted Elspeth King.
She texted back: 'put away they dustpans,
girls, get out the mallets, crowbars, chisels.'

Women's Timber Corps, 1942–46
'Lumberjills' bronze, 2007, Malcolm Robertson

The Museum of Women
(transcribed from Gaby Porter)

every manufactured object
can be viewed
as an article of production, consumption, use

women are seated in the parlour
appear as dummies in costume displays
domestic servants, shop assistants, occasionally
as munitions workers, but more usually
doing the laundry, cooking in the kitchen
surrounded by interesting but obsolete gadgetry
rather than sets of working tools

there is no study of the home as workplace

they are silent, women
even when they are singing

Rosettes in suffragette colours
in Votes for Women Exhibition, Museum of Edinburgh, 2010

(warning)
The management reserves the right
To alter the programme of events
Historical narratives, bouncy castles
Displays, anachronisms, without warning

Women's Social and Political Union (WSPU) sashes
green, purple, white, Edinburgh, 1909

purple stands for the royal blood that flows
through the veins of every suffragette,
white for purity in private and public life,
green is the colour of hope, emblem of spring

our past should not limit our future

Still a Gude Cause banner, 1909–2009, WEA:
WSPU, Women's Freedom League, Women's Suffrage Societies

we are sustained by the thing itself
its superb difficulty
braced by the beauty of what we are attempting
curiously buoyant

THE MUSEUM OF EDINBURGH

The north-east Edinburgh twilight
enters the town-house dwelling,
groaning with gear, the stuff of
Old Town living, silverware,
dummies peering round corners,
alcoves, the gasps tourists make,
as they turn, hear the sound their
own feet make travelling along
timbers, wooden floors, as they've
always done, as they always will,
as they look out of windows,
catch sight of Robert Fergusson's
pavement figure dashing between
bedlam and the Scottish Poetry Library.

Robert Fergusson, 2004
David Annand (b.1948)

THE MUSEUM OF MONEY

money is no object
in here

the beast beckons
you enter its lair

tread carpets
deep-red with knowing

you stare at
the machinery of wealth

the machinery of wealth
stares back

a million banknotes scream in their cage

Display case, a million banknotes
Museum on the Mound, Edinburgh

the last duel in Scotland took place
at Kirkcaldy in 1826 between a banker
and a dissatisfied customer
the banker died

Adam Smith, 2008, High Street, Edinburgh
Sandy Stoddart (b.1959)

the labour of menial servants is unproductive,
creates no commodities,
like that of the sovereign, officers of justice and war,
churchmen, lawyers, physicians, men of letters, musicians

ADAM SMITH

designing a banknote involves
an evocation of national identity

Iron kist
purchased by the Bank of Scotland, 1701, for £7.10d (£600)

Fell source o' a' my woe and grief!
For lack o' thee I've lost my lass!
For lack o' thee I scrimp my glass!
For lack o' thee, I leave this much-lov'd shore.

ROBERT BURNS, 'LINES WRITTEN ON A BANKNOTE', 1786

BIG DONALD

a big drink of water
Big Donald
trade-mark specs
crumpled suit
Bobby Charlton
hair-style
cake-stand legs
failing to convince
even themselves
they will fit in
as he sits there
munching buns
anything sweet
or fattening
except for him
Big Donald
a brain-box
filled with tricks
mouth racing
trying to outrun
its own intelligence
Big Donald
cool & quick
a big drink of water

Donald Dewar, 2002
Kenneth MacKay (b.1966)

it landed here
dead of night
an oblong space
a Georgian tardis
paid for by
the tobacco trade
darkies' tears
for which we all
still bear the gree
equal partners in
Britain's brutal Empire
towards which
the Saturday Art Club
may not seem that much
but it's a start
a step towards
the non colonial
the socially just
creative imaginings
nurtured here
inside this square
this welcome
geometric building

Seven and Seven is or Sunshine Bathed the Golden Glow, 2008
Jim Lambie (b.1964)

burds claim their freedom
and I'm for the burds

GEORGE WYLIE

Flat Iron Swan, welded metal and paint
George Wylie (b.1921)

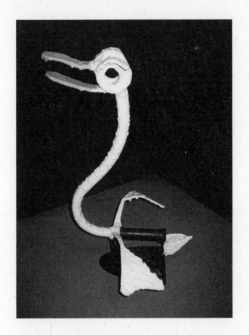

I prefer miscalculations
because they offer more promising results
you've got to know
how to busk yourself out of things

GEORGE WYLIE

momento mori
eyebrows waxened
nude
recumbent
despicable
fringed silk linings
looks of ecstasy
anatomically correct
encased in glass
commodified
uncertain

To Be Continued, 1976
John Byrne (b.1940)

they used to be called shopkeepers
you know
anyway
they're now called gallerists

JOHN BYRNE

THE 4TH PLINTH

anything is art if you say it is
Gilbert & George
two blokes on a plinth
living sculptures
whatever they do
whatever they say
is sculpture
concept is king
you no longer need to make anything
at all
they dance
they make music
animals can't do that

leave it empty

Ensign Ewart tomb, Sergeant at Waterloo, captured a French Standard
Edinburgh Castle esplanade, 1938

the people, yes
the people and the people's cause
Burke's *hoi poloi* the great unwashed
by bloodied fields and Combination Acts
by the handkerchief on which was stitched
'Scotland Free or A Desart' 1820
carried by James Wilson the Radical
his headless corpse his pauper's grave
by such was made
the people and the people's cause
their banners
inscribed waved planted

Keir Hardie, bronze statuette, 1957
Benno Schotz (1891–1984)

this question of loss
the pending history of
utopian disappointments
spectres and sputniks
overshadows everything

'The People's Happiness is the Statesman's Honour' banners
Edinburgh, 1838–48

I am not deceived.
You might have condemned me
without this mummery of a trial.
You want a victim. I will not shrink.

JAMES WILSON (speech from the dock)

Scotland's history has greed,
social inequality, injustice, the oppression
of women, children, other races, bigotry

Bludgeon, clarinet
carried at the Edinburgh Chartist Riot, Pilrig, 1848

if only they had had it (the vote, 1832)
it would give food, clothing, shelter
... there would now be a third change
– a struggle against capital

ERNEST JONES

COMIC FIGURES

Nothing ever changes, foreigners are funny,
the clock stopped at 1910, curiously archaic,
if working class characters do appear, then
it's usually as comics, acrobats, cowboys...

So Orwell summed them up, 'Boys Weeklies',
where misfortune is always individual,
and down to wickedness, not class, poverty
or 'the system' – which explains *Desperate Dan*.

Where does Dan come from? Dundee?
You think? Can you see Dan in the thirties
working in the mills? Minnie, different case,
a factory lass, out on the razz with the girls.

But Desperate Dan? An urban cowboy,
without a horse? A deluded pot-biler? I blame
DC Thomson, quick enough to sue a cartoon,
an 'Alternative Broons', in Thatcher's time,

in which the Twins are gay, Daphne a lesbian,
and Grandpaw, a Red Clydesider, a freend o'
John Maclean (no Jim, are you insane!). So,
Dundee, if you are listening, raise monuments

to all your greatest radicals, subversives:
McGonagall, Brooksbank, Mara, Galloway
(even Hamish McAlpine) – and then the
crowds will come, yea, even in their thousands.

Desperate Dan, 2001
Tony and Susie Morrow

GLESGA POLIS (GLASGOW POLICE MUSEUM)

'Di yi wa-ant ti see thi boadie?'
Ah, *Taggart*, Tartan-noir,
Mark McManus, voice, face, hair
sculpted in gravel, an unhappy
Sir Alex Ferguson, five-nil down,
half-time looming, the dressing-room,
the cell, in which Sir Arthur Conan Doyle's
Sherlock greets McIlvanney's *Laidlaw*,
the Glasgow existentialist, zen-calvinist,
whisky-priest, judge-penitent, dispensing
smoke and metaphor, Sartre and de Beauvoir,
in the corner, getting pissed. I wrote to him,
McIlvanney. He wrote straight back: 'your
letter came like a bandage for a sair day.'

Police Box, Buchanan Street, Glasgow

we live in a time
when our relationship to objects
is undergoing a radical transformation

Miniature police box, figure
Glasgow Police Museum

The newspaper-seller stands in Leith Walk,
a high sing-song voice and a good knowledge
of what sells newspapers: 'Read all about it!
Fucking terrible murder!'

there will be no bevvying

City of Glasgow Police Woman's uniform, c.1948

I think the *Big Man* fails as a film
because the boxing-match, a metaphor
for class-struggle in the novel,
becomes an 'event', not a relationship

art may be too important
to be left to the artists
but those who presume to comment
must learn to think like artists
not journalists or politicians

City of Glasgow Police Sergeant's uniform, c.1890

to insist on this rebellion
to enlarge the repertoire
the never tried, the new
to set the whole world on fire

LITTLE SPARTA

The horror! Imagine the Rates Department,
Strathclyde Regional Council, circa 1978,
getting a letter, the umpteenth that week,
from a citizen of an imagined country,
somewhere near Biggar, declaring itself
Independent (Norman MacCaig with knobs-on,
since Norman only declared *himself* Independent,
and always paid his rates).

MI6 would have been unworried, knowing
full-well the neighbouring realm of Brownsbank
was no longer part of an experimental artistic alliance,
having declared the poetry of the new state 'crap'.

Undaunted, imagine a young Rates Inspector,
having drawn the short-straw for the umpteenth
time that week, being waved off by his colleagues
to serve notice on yet another Situationist,
hiding in a byre – sorry temple – sorry gallery.

And the amazing thing is, it still exists,
unlike Strathclyde Regional Council.

A Man of Letters RLS, headstone & trees monument, 1987
Princes St Gardens, Ian Hamilton Finlay (1925–2006)

CONTEMPORARY ART
(transcribed from Anthony Caro)

let it talk to you
the stuff

putting it raw
into the gallery
off the street

you come to it
it comes to you
a question of going with it
a way into

the memory of paper
shattering the object
something about war
or the mutilations of war
to get in touch with it
its spirit

art is not the meat
art is about us
and being alive
and living in freedom

not did you sell anything

Still, 2004, Old St Paul's Edinburgh
Alison Watt (b.1965)

a quilt was the work of one woman
or several
worked and reworked until exhausted
worn away to nothing

museums of the moving image
museums without walls
museums without objects

HD video projection screen, the Centre for Contemporary Arts
Sauchiehall Street, Glasgow

private meditation
drowned out by
the whirr and clatter of
the audiovisual display

this link with capital
the focus on the present
the obliteration of the past
the rapid play of images
the erosion of historical memory
the mobility of objects and bodies
the development of free trade
the forgetting of politics, money, difference

Self-Portrait as a Drowned Man (The Willows)
2011, Jeremy Millar

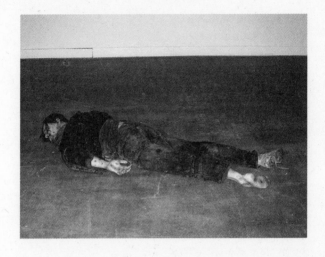

museums look at object-rich activities
such as cooking and serving
but overlook the laborious tasks
such as washing-up

MONUMENTS IN THE STREET

I love the way Mayakovsky
(visiting Paris in 1922)
personifies the Eiffel Tower.
Tower, he says, the Metro's
with us – will you take the lead?

All we need now's the explosives
and a team of Hamish Hendersons
to blow apart not pillar boxes
but plinths anyone on a horse
who fought to keep

the Empire monumental
beggared their neighbours
and never thought it dreadful
boom! and another one goes
boom! and another one goes

making way for
Mary Brooksbank's millsong
Jimmy Reid's electoral address
Sorley MacLean's honouring
England's little war-dead manikins

who brought such weeping to his eyes
and mine – so let us keep them human size
pavement figures breaking-stride
having our pictures taken with them
laughing and shaking hands

Lobey Dosser, Elfie, & Rank Bajin, 1992
Tony Morrow and Nick Gillan

THE MUSEUM OF CHILDHOOD

You're walking through the *Beano*
and the *Dandy*, scuffed-knees
rubbing shoulders with the attic toys
of cloistered Edwardian children,
Lord Snooty's pedal-car, lonely as
that doll's house, mansion-sized,
perfect in every detail, the parlour
maids, the rocking-horse, handmade,
by those who could not give them to
their own, the baby wear, the Sunday
toys, a hundred kinds of money-box, nose
pressed flat against the case, just out of
reach, a thousand dinky cars, train-sets,
each one a perfect replica, miniatures,
the manufactured bric-a-brac of empire,
trade, until, there, in the corner, a doll
made for a child in a London slum, 1911,
from an old shoe, studs for a mouth, eyes,
then up the winding stair to a circus,
an Arizona holster-set, like the one you
never got for Christmas, 1952, and
the silver-colts that sparkle on the lid.

Little Boys, presented by Heathrow Airports Authority Ltd PLC, 1994
Graham Ibbeson (b.1951)

these are our people in here
the dead
druids' cloaks
arthritic bones
rooms stuffed with photographs

chapels of remembrance
the once loved

Doll made from an old shoe, London, 1911

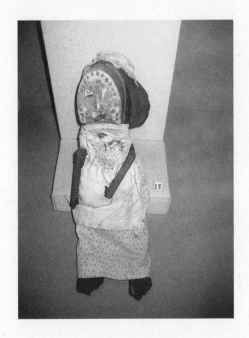

the court is its play-ground
the gutter its school-room
and under the care of an elder sister
the little one passes the day

a warhorse
a flat canvas with colours
arranged in a certain order
a painting

Galloper Horse from a roundabout, c.1902, Anderson of Bristol
maker of carved ship figureheads

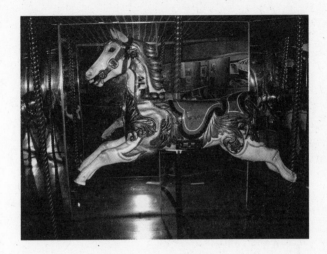

there are people at Ford
who specialise in handles
just as Rembrandt's studio called upon
specialist ruff painters and sword-renderers

THE FIVE SISTERS

Frae the Black Isles and the Borders
twa centuries ago
they laboured roond the Calders
above grund and ablo
and there was no idle bread.

O thir faithers they wir bastards and
thir grandfaithers they say
and ivry man a mason grand
no godless Irish they, o no
but I still remember them

mair braw nor aw the pharaohs
and aw thir chariats horse
and burnished by the burning blaes
– but who will sing for these
the slaves of ancient Egypt?

O ye dochters o' Jerusalem
raise up yir voices sing
men gaithered fire in thir airms
t'wrocht cathedrals for thir kings.

The Five Sisters shale-bing, West Calder, national monument

THE MUSEUM OF INDUSTRY
(SUMMERLEE HERITAGE PARK)

The iron gates say *in memoriam*
for all those killed by capital,
waged-labour, the forge, the mill,
the acrid fumes, the silent dust,
the hammering din, the rasp and thrust
of metal, the batons falling on a man,
arms entangled in machinery, the skills,
the craft of women, the raucous cries of
playing children, forty to a class, the tawse,
the coal-belts these gave way to, the wars,
more steel, more hammering, more smoke,
more backs broken, until, at last, it stopped,
was still, the work and joy, and now
these iron railings, these mammoth silent furnaces.

Two Coal Miners, bronze, 2001, Brandon Gate, Hamilton
Morag Farquharson (b.1953)

in thrall to
their empires, their interests, their beliefs

Coal hutch, c.1950s

Crawlin' aboot like a snail in the mud,
Covered wi' clammy blae,
Me, made after the image o' God –
Jings! But it's laughable tae.

a bustling market
dark smoky houses
and a busy wharf
see smell and hear
exactly what it was like
ignoring work, hunger, disease, war, death

Two Trade Unionists, 1986
Ken Currie (b.1960)

step aboard a time car
and be whisked back
through the centuries
to real-life Viking Britain

he who fights too long against dragons
becomes a dragon himself

Police whipping bench, c.1890–1950s
used for petty offences

the public prefer Bi-planes
to all the instruction in the world
Water-whorls, Witching-waves
Waggle-woggles and Flip-flaps

STATUES
(transcribed from James Fenton)

statues have been objects of horror
smashed by the mob
raised up by the connoisseur
gouged out of the mountainside
dropped in the sea
dragged the length and breadth of Europe
fought over by princes
made the journey to the Louvre

the Greeks had a word for statues
they called them *agalmata*
which meant things wherein one delights
and a sculptor was an *agalmatopoios*
a maker of delightful things

these statues that we have
these plucky survivors
escaping those who burned marble
for lime – an achievement
to have been dug up with respect
to not have met with the restorer's chisel

Headless Living Sculpture, 2011, Castlehill, Edinburgh

SURGEONS' HALL, EDINBURGH

This place helps you understand why
Dr Finlay's bag contained little more than
a stirrup-pump and a hammer – and by
the look of James Young Simpson's probe
no wonder his patients were all grateful for
the chloroform, before he inserted a spanner
in their works – for what a musket-ball
might do to a testicle is rather unimaginable –

or was, until you step in here, o dear,
just caught sight of something radical
that's been removed, it says, from someone
else's clavicle, o please, give me air,
but do not call a doctor, at least, not these,
to keep me back from death's dark welcoming republic.

From here, Health, 1994, Denys Mitchell

the dead rise from their coffins
objects come to life in their glass case

Cast from nature, 1845

John Goodsir (1814–67) FRCS Edinburgh, Professor of Anatomy

Oh to be at Crowdieknowe
When the last trumpet blaws,
An' see the deid come loupin' owre
The auld grey wa's.

HUGH MACDIARMID

the rawness of something
direct from the source
unpolished
not worked over

Fergusson's foot
Sir William Fergusson (1808–1877)

where the paper trail peters out
DNA steps in
confirming where we came from
the Caledonian forest, not kings

remember
when you speak of our failings
the dark time too
which you have escaped

The Blacksmith Dentist, anonymous

art is what makes our lives
a dead-end
a path to exile
a steep staircase

PATRICK GEDDES: THE SCOTS MORRIS

Then I taught them the crafts of metals,
and the sailing of the sea,
And the taming of the horse-kind,
and the yoke-beast husbandry,
And the building up of houses;
and that race of men went by,
And they said that Thor had taught them;
and a smything carle was I –
the best thing, poetically, William Morris
ever wrote, I'd say, the title alone
– Sigurd the Volsung – worth the price of
admission, though the rest of the poem,
complete crud. Anyway, Patrick Geddes,
like Morris, made arts & crafts & beauty vital.

Ramsay Gardens (not from Princes Street), 1890–93
Patrick Geddes (1854–1932)

we know too much about Bill Clinton's sex life
the drug problems of Britney Spears

East London Street Chapel murals, Edinburgh, 1893–1901
Phoebe Anna Traquair (1852–1936)

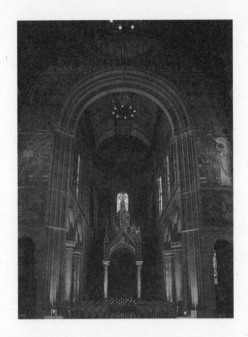

through the old town, so oft aflame,
the phoenix is once more fluttering,
and the doves rest once more
on St Margaret's chapel pinnacle

PATRICK GEDDES, 'The Scots Renascence'

museums show
there are alternative ways of organising societies

Glasgow School of Art, 1897–1909
Charles Rennie Mackintosh (1868–1928)

to make accessible the rarely seen
to unite comparable worlds
to alter or enhance perceptions
to get visitors through the turnstiles

JOHN KNOX'S GRAVE

I lie here in truth, cobbled under cars
kisted beneath a wee painted sign, a tile

a mark for tourists to gawk at
barristers run by, and dogs to sniff, aye

but I care not, I'm with the Lord
in Her many Mansions, we talk, I say,

see yon wee Japanese guy wi' the camera
standing where my thrapple used tae be

make his negatives disappear, o how we laugh
in Heaven, we've something special planned

for Bush and Blair, an exploding cigar perhaps
in the shape of Iraq, and when they say

we didnae ken, we'll say, well ye ken noo,
that's whit ye cry Scotch Education, aye

an auld yin, true, but it's still true the day.
My statue glowers outside St Giles, finger

pointing, ignored by all except the pigeons
who, thankfully, are not all Celtic fans.

The cars leak diesel on my cobbled stones
whit's new! – it's Saturday in Embro, Hearts

are at hame, and God's no pleased wi' you!

John Knox's grave, marked by a yellow tile, Parliament Square
Edinburgh, car parking space 23

SWEET SINGERS
(GREENHILL COVENANTERS' HOUSE)

Even Cargill, the leading light, could do nothing
with them, the Sweet Singers, a Bo'ness sect,
mainly women, four of them lost last week,
flung over the side of the gallows
in the Grassmarket, singing psalms,
as Cargill would when his time came
soon enough. He went to Gibb, their leader,
a huge ship's captain, on the Pentland muir.
Ever tried reasoning with a Taliban?
They'd send Gibb to America later,
when the dream turned to nightmare,
everything denounced, not just monarchy, but
storybooks and ballads, romances and pamphlets,
'and all the customs of this generation', they wrote,
from the Canongate tollbooth, their death cell,
'we renounce'. Who does not now tremble before
such certainty, in the smoke and utter ruin,
Edinburgh Old Town, 1681?

Female Covenanter, fireplace, 17th century
Greenhill Covenanters House, Biggar

museums are instruments of memory
memory on the scale of a huge wooden box

Scots press bed slept in by Donald Cargill, 12 July 1681;
hanged 27 July 1681

he thrashes about in the pulpit
bends over all sides
bangs his fist on the edge
stamps like a cavalry horse and shouts

MICHAEL MCGAHEY'S PORTRAIT
Maggi Hambling

Not for you full Highland regalia,
Clan Chief sporran, kilted Monarch of the Glen,
garb of some Public Schoolboy Robber Baron,
capital sunk in South African diamond mines, off-
    shore
scams, grouse-moors, the whole Victoriana
    pantomime.
You sit four-square, unblinking and, a little odd,
shirt collar unstraying, National Health specs not
    there,
but still, you wear the respectable suit of your class –
worn too by Lenin, and John Maclean, your father's
red blood coursing through your veins, for he too was
an aristocrat – of labour, a foundation member of the
    British
Communist Party – who thought you a compromiser,
    and
you agreed, for so too was Gallacher, who said: 'we are
a movement, not a monument'. You led with your
    head,
a marvellous orator, steeped in literature, gravel-
    voiced,
whose aim was a republic, here, in this place, built,
as you were, on brains, commonsense and laughter.

My Ties with Mick, 2004 Scottish National Portrait Gallery
Shelagh Atkinson (b.1959)

THE PEOPLE'S PALACE AND WINTER GARDEN

no crowding allowed, no standing in the passages
no vexatious extra charges
Family night every Friday
Sweethearts and Wives admitted free
Special stair reserved for ladies and children
Lavatories on every floor
The Boxing Kangaroo and the Wrestling Lion
Charity is not in our line
but change for a shilling is
with a spice of civility thrown in
We should have a dozen such Palaces

(Programme for the People's Palace music hall, 1894)

People's Palace and Winter Gardens, Glasgow, 1893–8
Alexander Beith MacDonald (1847–1915)

wrenched from the grasp of collective amnesia
oppositional history
necessary for the abolition of the status quo

Desk of John Maclean, purchased 1917

MacLean was not naïve, but

'we are out

for life and all that life can give us'

was what he said, that's what he said

EDWIN MORGAN

a banknote has to convince us
it is worth more than the paper it is printed on

Jimmy Reid: Seventy-Five Years, 2007
Barry Atherton (b.1944)

reject these attitudes
a rat race is for rats
we're not rats
we're human beings

the poignancy of objects
stepping stones towards feelings

about antiquity
the beauty of craftsmanship

the macabre
and a thousand other attributes

Baby prison clothes, made from prison uniforms and blankets, 1920s

we shall restore them to their true selves
against their will
we must begin with the rod
love will follow the disciplining

I rake through Angus Calder's essays –
looking for the photograph, of him and
George Gunn at MacDiarmid's Memorial,
on the hill above Langholm – 'Revolving
Culture: Notes from the Scottish Republic'
then, 'Scotlands of the Mind', then I
realise it was their expedition to scatter
Hamish Henderson, and there they are,
banner stretching between them, Gramsci's
head looking remarkably like MacDiarmid
in specs. Freud calls this 'screen memory',
one suppressing deeper fears, like the death
of Scottish international Republicanism?
My eye travels to the article Angus wrote on
Ken Currie, the influences on him: Rivera,
Mayakovsky, Eisenstein, Brecht, MacDiarmid.

Hamish Henderson's Gramscian send off, Ben Gulabin, Glenshee
2002, Timothy Neat (b.1943)

DUMFRIES MUSEUM AND CAMERA OBSCURA

to see the sky astronomically
and the Cumberland mountains close up
through an eight inch reflecting lens
the Gregorian telescope was bought
and the Camera Obscura for £100.10/-
the old stone windmill converted
large windows installed, a spiral stair
and when the townsfolk came they saw
before photography, cinema, television
amazing scenes strung on flickering light
to a darkened room, ships unloading cargoes
horse and cattle markets on Whitesands
and even Queensberry, the *Dumfries Courier*
declared, could be studied under every aspect

Hugh MacDiarmid Memorial, 1985
Jake Harvey (b.1948)

art can always survive the contingent
because twinge and fringe are all art comes from
to make significance out of the muck of our lives
as now, from stone and the random squawk of birds

James Hogg's curling stone, 1835
silk mourning dresses, c.1860–80s

Sweat, greybeards!
Concentrate. Sweep
hard, harder –
we might / yet win.

in a museum of photography
do you include the equipment
as well as the prints
and if so does this threaten
the status of photography as art
this taxonomic quandary
art or not
the art/technological divide
works by unnamed hands
seen differently from known 'masters'
the conferring of status and value
tainted with cultural elitism

Spiers glove knitting machine, steam powered, c.1900

imagine you are a hoover
in a second-hand shop window
write a poem
in the voice of the hoover

an object should not come
with an extensive instruction manual

shape should explain itself

Recent addition, umbrella stand, 2010

the old Janus-headed
to instruct or to please
has given way to
places for mindless gawping

CRASH BANG WALLOP

See them, waiting for the shutter to drop,
grim-faced, moustachioed, standing like
the James Bhoys, waiting to get shot
by a Mexican firing-squad, not quite sure
which side the heart is on, all legging'd up,
like pitmen, like Hiberno-Scottish Samurai,
Clyde-built, iron-cast, stoppers all, Barney
Battles, knee-length shinguards and two
shilpit wingers facing thirty-six inch thighs,
braced, ready to do or die for Brother Walfrid's
Poor Children's Charity Dinners – till they too
were booted out the park – once the money-men
arrived, the stands got built, the forty thousand
gates, the shares and dividends and the players'
back-handers (a pub for their captain, John Kelly,
Scotland's greatest ever player) and all went on,
playing under gas-light.

The Celtic team in 1888:
white strip, green collar, red badge with a green Celtic cross

CINEMA PARADISO

Tully's on the wing
Fernie, Peacock, a cross comes in
McGrory heads against the bar
the bar breaks
Larsson, Gemmell, Johnstone
Murdoch slams it past

Half-time: 1–0

Hood kicks off
McGrain, Evans, Simpson's out the box
McNeill punts it up the park
Yogi turns, dribbles
Dalglish, a wee dink
Harold Brattbakk's through – a bye

Full-time: 10–0

Stein stands
applauds the players
the crowd stands
roars

the cameras flash
the newsmen phone their papers

Jimmy Johnstone, bronze, 2008
Kate Robinson (b.1965)

THE IBROX STAIR DISASTER

the names of the dead
stretcher parties

you couldn't believe it
his belt

the small of his back
the things that stick in your mind

the significance
the loss suffered

their family their friends
their mates

those who survived
they all walked here together

impossible to convey
the feeling

Ibrox Disaster Memorial, John Greig statue, 2001
Andy Scott (b.1964) and Alison Bell (b.1960)

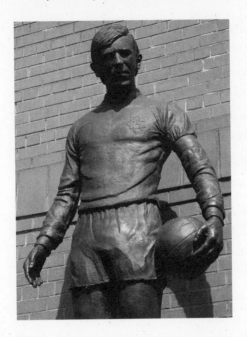

WAR ART

the machine-gun triumphed
modern yet primitive

artillery the last word in force
a predator searching for prey

a squat toad about to spit fire
a carcass still dripping with blood

the dead have to be remembered
without romanticising war

the return of the figurative
the body as a place

no more gods or heroes
an everyman we can project onto

our deepest human needs

The Drummer Boy, Winchburgh War Memorial, 2001, Alan Herriot

the bronze casts of the great statues of Rome
became field guns, sons of guns, grandsons of cannons

Half-moon battery cannon, 1573–88, artillery fortification
Edinburgh Castle War Memorial

I saw a great warrior of England,
a poor manikin on whom no eye would rest;
no Alasdair of Glen Garry;
and he took a little weeping to my eyes.

SORLEY MACLEAN, 'Heroes'

THE MUSEUM OF THE MIND
(transcribed from David Shields)

the lifespan of a fact is shrinking
a fact once lasted for as long as a kingdom stood
a legacy lived or a myth survived
its sceptics

facts have now dwindled
to the length of a generation
to the spans and memories of wars
plagues and depressions

the earth was once flat
but now we say it is round
a mere speck of dust
in a vast chaotic jumble

we remember what suits us
and there is almost no limit
to what we are able to forget

uss Enterprise NCC–1701 model
James Doohan Memorial Exhibition, Annet House, Linlithgow

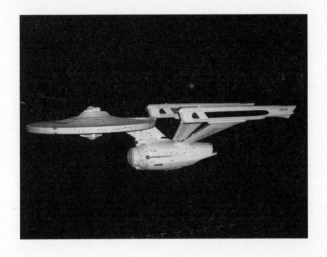

SCOTLAND'S GASWORKS

Even the Queen smiled at my opening,
well, a quarter of the Scottish vote
is Tory, and half of Labour's unionist,
but at least Big Tam was there, Connery,
and Donald, gangling, made his greatest
ever speech, Alex Salmond in the rear,
also smiling, the only visionary we've left,
in here, and, true to form, Burns the Radical,
was let out for the day, and soared,
then put in his box again, for another century,
ah weel, who gives a fart for culture anyway,
apart from the Arts Committee structure,
five Chairs in five years, one sacked for – eating pies.

Scottish Parliament building, 2004
Enric Miralles (1955–2000)

a room of sculpture
a cold confusion reigns
a dazzling bust appears
between the legs of a bronze athlete

David Hume, 1997, High Street, Edinburgh
Sandy Stoddart (b.1959)

my first posting was an assistantship
in the region of windswept borders
where I gave good calligraphy
in the third war of pointless encroachment

this object
not any other
not a clone
not a perfect replica
not anything else but this
in which Bonnie Prince Charlie himself stood
some 350 years ago
above marketing, entertainment, business
the authentic petticoats of Flora MacDonald

Travelling the Distance, 2007, Scottish Parliament
Shauna McMillan (b.1971)

we are changing this ill-divided world
we women o' vision
o' independent mind
bissums wi' smeddum

no area of culture
is immune to art's invasion

though there is as yet
no sustained interest in

darts or pigeon-fancying
recast as a shopping experience

Annie and Snow, from Fancy Pictures, 2008, Scottish Parliament
Mark Neville (b.1966)

If a man tells me that his family
came over with the Normans
I say 'Yes, very interesting;
and are you liking it here?'

all modern states are artefacts
based on conquest and colonisation
and a laboriously created national identity

Writer's Wall, Scottish Parliament building

I can no longer remain in this building.
Huge opposing armies disappear within it.
The next morning, the priests tentatively re-emerge.
Unable to sleep, I turn the bedside lamp on.

Just a moment, I'm chairman here.
I decide who speaks. (D Daiches)
That's the trouble with Scotland.
There's always a bloody chairman. (A Trocchi)

EDINBURGH WRITERS' CONFERENCE, 1962

Hamish Henderson, head, 2003, Edinburgh Park
Tony Morrow (b.1950)

If a man were permitted
to make all the ballads
he need not care
who should make the laws of a nation.

the sitters are there
in all their particularity
and we can study them

it is impossible to imagine them
considering us

Poets' Pub, 1980, Scottish National Portrait Gallery
Sandy Moffat (b.1943)

Scottish nationalism
a tiny movement
motivated by sentiment
inspired by distilleries

we must redesign our discourses
loosen the dependence of change upon calamity
lighten the burdens of poverty, inequality, drudgery

Mary Queen of Scots, 2002, Annet House garden, Linlithgow
Tom McGowran (1918–2001)

ancient Scotland was never Queen Mary
it's those serfs they kept chained
in the Fifeshire mines
a hundred years ago

LEWIS GRASSIC GIBBON

I AM ELIZABETH, JOHN KNOX'S DAUGHTER

I am Elizabeth, John Knox's daughter
wife of John Welsh, minister of Ayr
who rebuked King James for cursing
and for banning the General Assembly
for which they banished him to France
on a trumpt up charge
my husband fought for the Huguenots
in the pulpit
and on the walls
his boldness a by-word
King Louis made him his minister
till, death approaching
we came back to London
to ask the King
to give him his native air
give him the Devil, he replied
unless he submit to the bishops
I, John Knox's daughter, Elizabeth
lifting my apron towards his majestie
declared I'd rather keep his heid in there
he died not long after, 1622,
and myself three years later, daughter
of my father, wife of my husband
in Ayr

The *Cutty Stool* (in memoriam Jenny Geddes, 1600–1660)
St Giles Cathedral, 1992, Merilyn Smith (b.1942)

my language is female coloured
as well as Scottish coloured

Liz Lochhead, head, 2005, Edinburgh Park
Vincent Butler (b.1933)

In *Memo From Spring* I found a woman poet
that also questioned language:
'women gossip, women natter,
men talk, men talk, men talk.'

JACKIE KAY

a nation is a group of people
united by a mistaken view of the past
and a hatred of their neighbours

The Vital Spark, puffer, 2006
George Wylie (b.1921)

my flag
is red
my country
the future

between pleasure and entertainment
the exploitative and the sincere
the ephemeral and the enduring
the hype and history
consumption and production
capital and culture
lie the museums

Songs of Scotland, book design, Talbot Rice Gallery Exhibition, 2010
Alasdair Gray (b.1934)

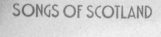

this already dated novel
is set inside the head of an aging,
divorced, alcoholic, insomniac,
tippling in the bedroom of a small Scottish hotel

ALASDAIR GRAY

animals painted as livestock
pieces of furniture with four legs
confirm the owner's pedigree

the owner's wealth more obvious
than the virtuosity of the artist

6 Definitions, Peace (inscription below), 2001, Dean Gallery grounds
Ian Hamilton Finlay (1925–2006)

n. according to St Ignatius of Loyola:
the simplicity of order.
War on the castles,
Peace to the cabins.

SLOGAN OF THE FRENCH REVOLUTIONARY ARMIES

lost in a turmoil
the chaos of sizes
dwarfs and giants
the finished
the restored
the incomplete

James Clerk Maxwell, 2008, George Street, Edinburgh
Sandy Stoddart (b.1959)

I wanted to be with men I admired
rather than the Scottish Arts Council crowd
so I spent a lot of time in graveyards.
You get less trouble from the dead.

SANDY STODDART

Our Museums
Tombs of the Pharaohs
Burial-ships of the Vikings
Trade Fairs of the Victorians
Machine Halls of the Workers
Aladdin's Caves of the Masses
Dust-carts of the Corporations
Shopping Malls of the Consumers
Punter-Disneyland-Heritage-Amusement-Arcades

Writing desk and chair of Robert Burns
Robert Burns Birthplace Museum, Alloway

listen to the tune, Master Robert, sit properly in your chair
– playing Hannibal crossing the Alps, in rapture,
up and down, with bagpipe and recruiting drum,
wishing myself tall enough to be a soldier

the Scottish Enlightenment introduced the fork,
the water closet, the handkerchief and night attire
to mediate, distance, conceal, the body's necessities

Twa Dugs, 2000, Calum Colvin (b.1961)

Rabbie's upstairs mowin' Cutty Sark
when Donald Findlay turns up, pits oan
'Marching Bands o' the British Army'
–- syne Ossian rips his hert oot.

**work as if you live
in the early days of a better nation**

Edinburgh Trades Council International Workers Memorial Day Tree
28 April, Princes St Gardens

For healthy and safe
working lives
Remember the dead
Fight for the living

(inscription)

we seek identity in history's celebrities
local histories, wars

but rarely, if ever
in the existence of a national cricket team

Portrait of Burns, 2001, Calum Colvin (b.1961)

the enemies of Scottish nationalism
are not the English
our real enemies are among us
those born without imagination

RB CUNNINGHAM GRAHAM

SOURCES

Many of the commentaries and quatrains of verse derive from the
collection of essays edited by Peter Vergo, *The New Museology*
(Reaktion Books, London, 1997), especially his Introduction and
essay 'The Reticent Object'. Ludmilla Jordanov's essay 'Objects of
Knowledge' is equally rich in observation and arresting detail.
The opening commentary 'beyond the captions' (p.3, 32) is in fact
a composite of phrases taken from both Vergo and Jordanov. Other
commentaries taken from Vergo include 'museums of the moving
image' (41), 'the aesthetic view' and 'reticent objects' (49), 'one small
item' and 'private meditation' (51), 'an object can stand for' (53) and
some of 'beyond the class system' (3). Ludmilla Jordanov largely
supplies 'in museums' and 'the poignancy of objects' (23), 'in a
museum of photography' (24), 'step aboard a time-car' and 'a
bustling market' (25) and 'momento mori' (35–6). Other essayists in
Vergo used include Colin Sorensen's 'Our Museums' (73); Charles
Saumerez Smith's 'the doorway' (12–15); Paul Greenhalgh's 'a
comprehensive display' (87) and 'the public prefer Bi-planes' (85);
Maurice Denis's 'a warhorse' (49).

I should add that this book is not itself an academic 'essay'
and I sometimes exercise 'poetic licence' regarding the sources by
adding or subtracting or inserting or combining or twisting or
reversing words, syntax and the like, though this is usually quite
marginal. Gaby Porter's essay 'Putting Your House in Order' in
Robert Lumley's *The Museum Time Machine* (Routledge, London, 1992)
provides most of the poem 'The Museum of Women' (106–7, 111, 115)
and 'a fascination with the way things work' (102), 'a quilt' (109) and
'museums look at object-rich activities' (112). Deyan Sudjic's *The*

Language of Things (Penguin, London, 2009) supplies 'our homes are filled' (5), 'what every designer wants' (53), 'designing a banknote' (71), 'there are people at Ford' (121), 'the history of the modern chair' (187), 'only wealthy women' (203) and 'we live in a time' (216). Cedric Watts & Lawrence Davies' *Cunninghame Graham: A Critical Biography* (Cambridge UP, London, 1979) supplies 'I believe that the people' (82), 'Niggers who have no cannons' (163), 'the enemies of Scottish nationalism' (255) and (their own observation) 'Scottish nationalism, a tiny movement' (248) while Ian M Fraser's *R.B. Cunninghame Graham: Fighter for Justice* (privately printed, Gargunnock, 2002) supplies 'Love of man' (66) and 'all the cares of life' (27). Margaret Macmillan's *The Uses and Abuses of History* (Profile Books, London, 2009) supplies 'we know too much' (19), 'where the paper-trail peters out' (7), 'a nation is a group of people' (82) and Heinrich von Treitschke's 'we shall restore them' (102).

John Berger's *Ways of Seeing* (BBC & Penguin, London, 2008) supplies 'the sitters are there' (92) and 'animals painted as livestock' (93). James Fenton's *Leonardo's Nephew* (Penguin, London, 1998) provides most of the poem 'Statues' (13, 15, 18) and also 'the bronze casts' (9). Rab Houston's *Scotland: A Very Short Introduction* (Oxford UP, New York, 2008) supplies 'the Scottish Enlightenment' (71) and 'the last duel in Scotland' (72). John Mack's *The Museum of the Mind* (British Museum Press, London, 2003) supplies 'museums are instruments' and 'art is what' (16) and 'the dead rise' (18). James Cuno's *Whose Muse?* (Princeton UP, New Jersey, 2004) supplies Neil MacGregor's 'the truth of cataloguing' (30–3) and Paul Valery's 'a room of sculpture' and 'lost in a turmoil' (53). Ian Grimble's *Highland Man* (Highlands & Islands DB, Inverness, 1980) is the source for the terms 'the stone-axe factories' (15) and 'mesolithic flint knappers' (34).

The following provide mainly single sources, running chronologically from Harold Alaric Jacob who supplies 'I would rather make a thin living in the arts' (73) in Christopher Norris's *Inside the Myth: Orwell, Views from the Left* (editor, Lawrence & Wishart, 1984); John Russell in Michael Peppiatt's *Francis Bacon* (Constable, 2008) supplies 'their anatomy half-human' (130); Mary MacPherson 'Big Mary of the Songs' poem in Sorley Maclean's *Ris a Bhruthaic* (ed. William Gillies, Acair, Stornoway, 1997) supplies 'and when I am in the boards' and 'and the 'beggars' of gentry' (74); Mrs Pethwick Lawrence, WSPU Suffragette, supplies 'purple stands for'; David Hare in *Obedience, Struggle & Revolt* (Faber & Faber, London, 2005) supplies 'we are sustained'; George Wylie display labels supply 'burds claim their freedom' and 'I prefer miscalculations'; John Byrne interview with Jennie Renton, 2008, online, supplies 'they used to be called shopkeepers'; James Wilson's speech from the dock in P. Berresford Elllis & Seumus Mac a Ghobhainn's *The Scottish Insurrection of 1820* (Gollancz, London, 1970) supplies 'I am not deceived' (255); Ernest Jones display label supplies 'if only they had had it'; Alasdair Paterson's *Brief Lives* (Oasis Books, London, 1987) supplies 'the newspaper-seller' (28) and his *on the governing of empires* (Shearsman Books, Exeter, 2010) supplies 'my first posting' (42); Simon Callow's *Being an Actor* (Penguin, London, 1985) supplies 'art may be too important' (85); Roberto Mangabeira Unger's *The Left Alternative* (Verso, London, 2009) supplies 'to insist on this rebellion' (VIII, XXII) and 'we must redesign our discourses' (61); an interview with Sir Anthony Caro on a BBC Four arts programme, 2010, supplies the poem 'Contemporary Art'; Henry Mayhew's *London Labour and The London Poor* (Penguin, London, 1987) supplies 'the court is its play-ground' (44); Joe Corrie's poem 'The Image O' God' in *Joe Corrie:*

Plays, Poems & Theatre Writings (7:84 Publications, Edinburgh, 1985) supplies 'crawlin' aboot like a snail' (138); Friedrich Nietzsche in *Beyond Good and Evil*, Aphorism 146, supplies 'he who fights too long against dragons'; Hugh MacDiarmid's poem 'Crowdieknowe' in *The Complete Poems, Volume 1* (ed. Michael Grieve and W.R. Aitken, Penguin, 1985) supplies 'Oh to be at Crowdieknowe' (26); Bertolt Brecht's poem 'To Those Born Later' in *Poems 1913–1956* (Methuen, 2000) supplies 'remember when you speak of our failings' (319); Patrick Geddes in 'The Scots Renascence' (*Edinburgh Review*, issue 88, Polygon, Edinburgh, summer 1992) supplies 'through the old town' (20); Friedrich Engels in Tristram Hunt's *The Frock-Coated Communist* (Penguin, London, 2010) supplies 'he thrashes about' (17); Elspeth King's *The People's Palace & Glasgow Green* (Chambers, Edinburgh, 1995) supplies the People's Palace Music-Hall Program, 1894, (17); Edwin Morgan's poem 'On John MacLean' in *Collected Poems* (Carcanet, Manchester, 1996) supplies 'MacLean was not naïve' (351); Jimmy Reid's Glasgow Rectorial Address, 1972, supplies 'reject these attitudes'; Angus Calder's poem 'Fringe Events' in *Colours of Grief* (Shoestring Press, Nottingham, 2002) supplies 'art can always survive the contingent' (VII) and 'Curling' in *Sun Behind the Castle* (Luath, Edinburgh, 2004) supplies 'Sweat, greybeards!' (37); Sorley Maclean's poem 'Heroes' in *From Wood to Ridge* (Carcanet, Manchester, 1989) supplies 'I saw a great warrior of England'; David Shields' *Reality Hunger* (Hamish Hamilton, London, 2010) (section 51) supplies most of the poem 'The Museum of the Mind' and, earlier, 'the rawness of something' (section 241); Esther Breitenbach in Panel 3 of 'Travelling the Distance', Scottish Parliament, supplies 'we are changing this ill-divided world'; Raymond Williams in Christopher Hitchens' *Unacknowledged Legislators* (Verso, London, 20002) supplies 'if a man tells me' (35); Frank Kuppner's poetry collection *The Intelligent Observation of Naked Women* (Carcanet, Manchester, 1987) supplies 'I can no longer remain' (9,47,92); David Daiches and Alexander Trocchi in Allan Campbell & Tim Neil's *A Life in Pieces* (Rebel Inc, Canongate, Edinburgh, 1997) supplies 'just a moment' (157); Andrew Fletcher of Saltoun supplies 'if a man were permitted to make all the ballads'; Lewis Grassic Gibbon's letter to Helen B Cruikshank, 1933, in William K Malcolm's *A Blasphemer and Reformer* (AUP, Aberdeen, 1984) supplies 'ancient Scotland' (6); Elish Angiolini on Liz Lochead in Panel 2 of 'Travelling the Distance', Scottish Parliament, supplies 'my language is female coloured'; Jackie Kay on Liz Lochhead, *Sunday Herald*, 6/3/2011, online, supplies 'In Memo for Spring'; George Galloway's *I'm Not The Only One* (Allen Lane, Penguin, London, 2004) supplies 'my flag is red' (74); Alasdair Gray's novel 1982, *Janine* (Canongate, Edinburgh, 2003) back-cover supplies 'this already dated novel'; Sandy Stoddart, *The Guardian*, 6/6/2009, online, supplies 'I wanted to be with men I admired'; Robert Burns Birthplace Museum labels and audio-tape provides 'listen to the tune, Master Robert'; Dennis Leigh supplies 'work as if you live'.

I identify some specific figures as sources in the text itself, mostly Scottish radicals, none more so than RB Cunninghame Graham who I consider a shamefully neglected cultural figure. Cunninghame Graham stretched his family's traditional radical Liberal allegiances to embrace Marxism in the 1880s–90s (admittedly a fluid movement at that point), notably backing Keir Hardie to the hilt in forming the Scottish Labour Party, the Independent Labour Party and then the Labour Party. For the Labour Party to become, and remain, 'socialist', Cunninghame Graham thought that its leadership should consist of working-class proletarians determined to remain independent of Liberal-Fabian politics and politicians. His disappointment at the failure of Ramsay MacDonald's Government to adhere to socialist principles in the 1920s, or to secure Home Rule for Scotland, spurred him into co-founding the National Party of Scotland with Hugh MacDiarmid in 1928. Being far too radical for either the labour and nationalist movements of his day may explain why it has been Cunninghame Graham's fate to be embraced by neither of these traditions. Now, erased from public memory and academic interest, RB Cunninghame Graham, the first campaigning socialist MP in Parliament, remains one of modern Scotland's best-kept cultural and political secrets. A brilliant literary stylist and an unashamedly cosmopolitan and internationalist figure, Cunninghame Graham, like Thomas Stuart Smith, the founder of the Stirling Smith Art Gallery & Museum, was strongly anti-Imperialist and anti-racist in outlook. The lines taken from his explosive essay, *Niggers*, with its trenchant condemnation of late Victorian Imperialism – 'Niggers who have no cannons' – thus supplies the 'voice' that accompanies Stuart Smith's painting, *Pipe of Freedom*, which, in terms of Scottish-British art is a rare, perhaps even unique, celebration of the abolition of slavery in America.

Luath Press Limited

committed to publishing well written books worth reading

LUATH PRESS takes its name from Robert Burns, whose little collie Luath (*Gael.*, swift or nimble) tripped up Jean Armour at a wedding and gave him the chance to speak to the woman who was to be his wife and the abiding love of his life. Burns called one of 'The Twa Dogs' Luath after Cuchullin's hunting dog in Ossian's *Fingal*. Luath Press was established in 1981 in the heart of Burns country, and now resides a few steps up the road from Burns' first lodgings on Edinburgh's Royal Mile.

Luath offers you distinctive writing with a hint of unexpected pleasures.

Most bookshops in the UK, the US, Canada, Australia, New Zealand and parts of Europe either carry our books in stock or can order them for you. To order direct from us, please send a £sterling cheque, postal order, international money order or your credit card details (number, address of cardholder and expiry date) to us at the address below. Please add post and packing as follows: UK – £1.00 per delivery address; overseas surface mail – £2.50 per delivery address; overseas airmail – £3.50 for the first book to each delivery address, plus £1.00 for each additional book by airmail to the same address. If your order is a gift, we will happily enclose your card or message at no extra charge.

Luath Press Limited
543/2 Castlehill
The Royal Mile
Edinburgh EH1 2ND
Scotland

Telephone: 0131 225 4326 (24 hours)
Fax: 0131 225 4324
Email: sales@luath.co.uk
Website: www.luath.co.uk